The Snail's Trail Block

A Classic For Today's Quilts

Building Blocks Series 1 — Book 4

Special thanks to the following
for the beautiful fabrics used
in the quilts in this book:

Exclusively Quilters

Henry Glass & Co.

P&B Textiles

Red Rooster Fabrics

Studio e Fabrics

All quilt designs by Sandy Boobar and
Sue Harvey of Pine Tree Country Quilts,
www.pinetreecountryquilts.com.

Published by

All American Crafts, Inc.
7 Waterloo Road
Stanhope, NJ 07874
www.allamericancrafts.com

Publisher | **Jerry Cohen**

Chief Executive Officer | **Darren Cohen**

Product Development
Director | **Brett Cohen**

Editor | **Sue Harvey**

Proofreader | **Natalie Rhinesmith**

Art Director | **Kelly Albertson**

Illustrations | **Kathleen Geary, Roni Palmisano
& Chrissy Scholz**

Product Development
Manager | **Pamela Mostek**

Vice President/Quilting Advertising
& Marketing | **Carol Newman**

Printed in China
ISBN: 978-1-936708-05-5
UPC: 793573035288

www.allamericancrafts.com

Contents
Table of Contents

Welcome

Welcome to the Building Blocks series of quilting books.

Whether you're making your first or your one hundred and first quilt, the eight books in this series will be an invaluable addition to your quilting library. Besides featuring the instructions for a different traditional and timeless block in each book, we've also included charts to give you all the quick information you need to change the block size for your own project.

Each book features complete instructions for three different quilts using the featured block with variations in size, color, and style—all designed to inspire you to use these timeless blocks for quilts with today's look.

The Finishing Basics section in each book gives you the tips and techniques you'll need to border, quilt, and bind the quilts in this book (or any quilt you may choose to make). If you're an experienced quilter, these books will be an excellent addition to your reference library. When you want to enlarge or reduce a block, the numbers are already there for you! No math required!

The blocks in the Building Blocks series of books have stood the test of time and are still favorites with quilters today. Although they're traditional blocks, they look very contemporary in today's bold and beautiful fabrics. This definitely puts them in the category of quilting classics!

For each block, you'll find a little background about its name, origin, or era, just to add a touch of quilting trivia. The block presented in this book is Snail's Trail. The pattern was published several times in the 1920s and 30s as Monkey Wrench, Indiana Puzzle, and Snail's Trail. Unless it was made with scraps, the block was always pieced with only two fabrics. Whether made of scraps or planned fabrics, two sides of the block were dark and two were medium or light.

The most popular traditional setting for a Snail's Trail quilt is to alternate the pieced blocks with light and dark solid squares. This makes a larger version of the twisting design of a block-to-block setting with less than half of the piecing and no matching from block to block. Early quilters knew how to simplify!

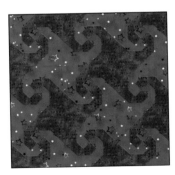 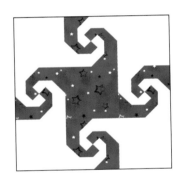

The Snail's Trail block offers so many different arrangements and secondary designs, and adds so much motion to a quilt, that it has never gone out of style. Three very different arrangements of the block in this book show just a few of the possibilities. Experiment with color placement, prints and solids, and brights and pastels in your blocks. Then turn them, add sashing or plain setting squares, or shake things up with a differ-ent pieced block. Let your imagination run wild!

Snail's Trai

se these instructions to make the blocks for the quilts in this book. The materials needed for each quilt and the cutting instructions are given with the pattern for the quilt. Also included is a Build It Your Way chart with four different sizes for this block and the sizes to cut the pieces for one block. Use this information to design your own quilt or to change the size of any of the quilts in this book.

BUILDING THE BLOCK

Use a 1/4" seam allowance throughout.

1. The easiest way to piece this block for the quilts in this book, or any quilt that uses more than just a few blocks, is to begin with strip sets to make the block center. Instructions are given in the pattern for each quilt that uses this method. Refer to those instructions and then continue with step 4.

2. To piece a single block or a small number of blocks, choose the block size from the Build It Your Way chart. Cut one of each square A—P for each block. Cut each E-P square in half diagonally to make two triangles from each square. You will use one of each letter triangle for each block.

3. Sew an A square to a B square. Press seam toward the B square. Sew a C square to a D square. Press seam toward the C square.

Sew the pieced strips together to complete the block center. Press seam in one direction.

Build It Better

Having trouble aligning the triangles with the squares? Align the corner of the triangle with the seam between the squares in the block center. The two sharp corners of the triangle should extend equally beyond the edges of the square.

4. Stitch an E triangle to the AB side of the block center and an F triangle to the CD side. Press seams toward the E and F triangles. Sew a G triangle to the BD side of the block center and an H triangle to the AC side. Press seams toward the G and H triangles to complete the first round of triangles.

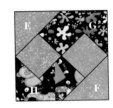

5. Sew an I triangle to the EG side and a J triangle to the FH side of the pieced unit. Press seams toward the triangles. Sew a K triangle to the FG side and an L triangle to the EH side of the pieced unit. Press seams toward the triangles to complete the second round of triangles.

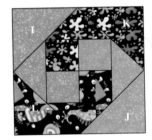

6. Stitch an M triangle to the IK side and an N triangle to the JL side of the pieced unit. Press seams toward the triangles. Sew an O triangle to the JK side and a P triangle to the IL side of the pieced unit to complete the Snail's Trail block. Press seams toward the triangles.

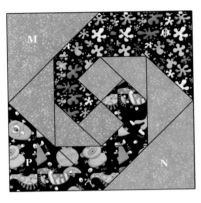

7. Repeat to complete the number of blocks needed for the quilt that you have chosen.

Build It Better

Trim off those dog ears to reduce bulk before moving on to the next sewing step.

Build It Your Way				
Piece	**5" Block**	**8¹⁄₂" Block**	**12" Block**	**17" Block**
A, B, C, D	1³⁄₈" x 1³⁄₈"	2" x 2"	2⁵⁄₈" x 2⁵⁄₈"	3¹⁄₂" x 3¹⁄₂"
E, F, G, H*	2¹⁄₈" x 2¹⁄₈"	3" x 3"	3⁷⁄₈" x 3⁷⁄₈"	5¹⁄₈" x 5¹⁄₈"
I, J, K, L*	2⁵⁄₈" x 2⁵⁄₈"	3⁷⁄₈" x 3⁷⁄₈"	5¹⁄₈" x 5¹⁄₈"	6⁷⁄₈" x 6⁷⁄₈"
M, N, O, P*	3³⁄₈" x 3³⁄₈"	5¹⁄₈" x 5¹⁄₈"	6⁷⁄₈" x 6⁷⁄₈"	9³⁄₈" x 9³⁄₈"
Cut in half diagonally to make 2 triangles per square				

Spyro Gyro

The twisting, turning antics of the Snail's Trail block stand out with the use of very different near-solids and prints. Each block looks like a little whirlpool spinning within its black frame. Placing sashing between the blocks takes all the work out of matching angled seams, making this a great design for a true beginner.

Finished Quilt Size: 71" x 90"
Finished Block Size: 17" x 17"
Number of Blocks: 12
Skill Level: Beginner

MATERIALS
All yardages are based on 42"-wide fabric.

❖ 1 1/4 yards of orange texture
❖ 2 5/8 yards black flower print
❖ 1 1/4 yards black monster print
❖ 1 1/4 yards of green texture
❖ 1 3/4 yards of black solid
❖ 1/4 yard of turquoise texture
❖ 5 5/8 yards of backing fabric
❖ 79" x 98" piece of batting
❖ Thread to match fabrics
❖ Rotary cutting tools
❖ Basic sewing supplies

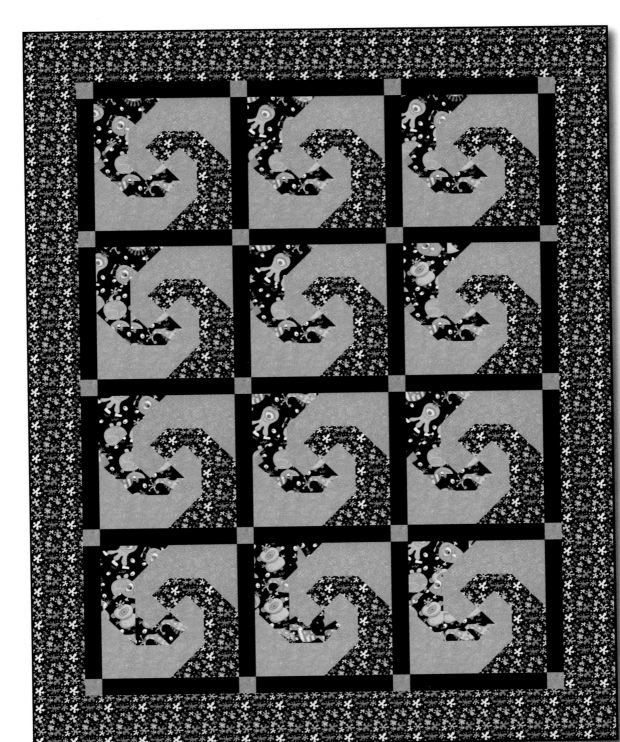

CUTTING

Label all pieces with the letters assigned. They will be used throughout the instructions.

From the orange texture, cut
- 1 A strip $3^1/2$" x 42"
- 1 strip $5^1/8$" x 42"; recut into (6) $5^1/8$" squares, then cut each square in half diagonally to make 12 E triangles
- 1 strip $6^7/8$" x 42"; recut into (6) $6^7/8$" squares, then cut each square in half diagonally to make 12 I triangles
- 2 strips $9^3/8$" x 42"; recut into (6) $9^3/8$" squares, then cut each square in half diagonally to make 12 M triangles

From the black flower print, cut
- 1 B strip $3^1/2$" x 42"
- 1 strip $5^1/8$" x 42"; recut into (6) $5^1/8$" squares, then cut each square in half diagonally to make 12 G triangles
- 1 strip $6^7/8$" x 42"; recut into (6) $6^7/8$" squares, then cut each square in half diagonally to make 12 K triangles
- 2 strips $9^3/8$" x 42"; recut into (6) $9^3/8$" squares, then cut each square in half diagonally to make 12 O triangles
- 8 strips $6^1/2$" x 42" for outer border

From the black monster print, cut
- 1 C strip $3^1/2$" x 42"
- 1 strip $5^1/8$" x 42"; recut into (6) $5^1/8$" squares, then cut each square in half diagonally to make 12 H triangles
- 1 strip $6^7/8$" x 42"; recut into (6) $6^7/8$" squares, then cut each square in half diagonally to make 12 L triangles
- 2 strips $9^3/8$" x 42"; recut into (6) $9^3/8$" squares, then cut each square in half diagonally to make 12 P triangles

From the green texture, cut
- 1 D strip $3^1/2$" x 42"
- 1 strip $5^1/8$" x 42"; recut into (6) $5^1/8$" squares, then cut each square in half diagonally to make 12 F triangles
- 1 strip $6^7/8$" x 42"; recut into (6) $6^7/8$" squares, then cut each square in half diagonally to make 12 J triangles
- 2 strips $9^3/8$" x 42"; recut into (6) $9^3/8$" squares, then cut each square in half diagonally to make 12 N triangles

From the black solid, cut
- 2 strips $17^1/2$" x 42"; recut into (31) $2^1/2$" x $17^1/2$" Q strips
- 8 strips $2^1/4$" x 42" for binding

From the turquoise texture, cut
- 2 strips $2^1/2$" x 42"; recut into (20) $2^1/2$" R squares

From the backing fabric, cut
- 2 pieces 98" long

MAKING THE SNAIL'S TRAIL BLOCKS

Note: *Use a $1/4$" seam allowance throughout unless otherwise instructed.*

1. Sew an orange A strip lengthwise together with a

black flower B strip. Press seam toward the B strip. Crosscut the strip set into (12) 3½" AB segments.

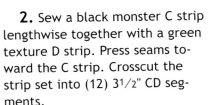

2. Sew a black monster C strip lengthwise together with a green texture D strip. Press seams toward the C strip. Crosscut the strip set into (12) 3½" CD segments.

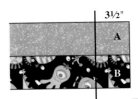

3. Sew an AB segment to a CD segment to complete a block center. Press seam to one side. Repeat to make 12 block centers total.

Make 12

4. Refer to Building the Block on page 6, steps 4-7, to make (12) 17½" x 17½" Snail's Trail blocks.

COMPLETING THE QUILT CENTER

1. Sew three blocks alternately together with four black solid Q strips to make a block row. Press seams toward the Q strips. Repeat to make four block rows total.

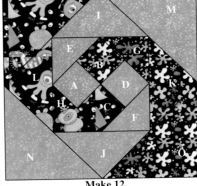

Make 12

2. Sew three black solid Q strips alternately together with four turquoise R squares to make a sashing row. Press seams toward the Q strips. Repeat to make five sashing rows total.

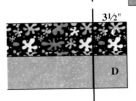

Make 5

3. Join the block rows and sashing rows alternately together to complete the 59½" x 78½" quilt center. Press seams toward the sashing rows. (Refer to the Quilt Assembly Diagram on page 12.)

4. Sew the 6½" x 42" black flower print strips short ends together to make a long strip. Cut into two 78½" strips and two 71½" strips. Sew the longer strips to the long sides and the shorter strips to the top and bottom of the quilt center to complete the quilt top. Press seams toward the strips. *Note: Refer to Finishing Basics on page 26 for information about cutting border strips.*

Build It Better

Go easy on the pressing! The 12 triangles in each Snail's Trail block mean plenty of chances to stretch the pieces with too heavy a hand when pressing. Remember, pressing is an up-and-down motion, not a back-and-forth motion. Flip the triangle to the right side and smooth it in place with your fingers, then bring your iron straight down onto the seam. Your seams will be nice and flat, with no distortion.

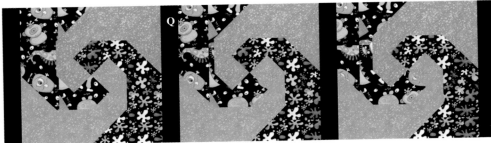

Make 4

FINISHING THE QUILT

1. Remove the selvage edges from the backing pieces. Sew the pieces together down the length with a $1/2$" seam allowance. Trim the sides to make a 79" x 98" backing piece. Press seam open.

2. Refer to Finishing Basics to layer, quilt, and bind your quilt.

Quilt Assembly Diagram

Make a darling baby quilt with 8½" blocks instead of the large blocks used in the original quilt. Cut 2" x 9" Q strips for sashing and 4½" x 42" strips for the outer border to make a 39" x 49" finished size.

Traditional Trails

Using only two fabrics for the "trails" is the more traditional way of piecing the Snail's Trail block. Set side by side, the blocks form tilted Friendship stars that fit into each other like the pieces in a crossword puzzle.

Finished Quilt Size: 64" x 64"
Finished Block Size: 12" x 12"
Number of Blocks: 16
Skill Level: Confident Beginner

MATERIALS
All yardages are based on 42"-wide fabric.

- ❖ 1/4 yard of light blue star print
- ❖ 1/4 yard of red texture
- ❖ 1 1/4 yards of medium blue print
- ❖ 1 3/4 yards of red star print
- ❖ 5/8 yard of stripe
- ❖ 1 1/4 yards of navy star print
- ❖ 4 1/4 yards of backing fabric
- ❖ 72" x 72" piece of batting
- ❖ Thread to match fabrics
- ❖ Rotary cutting tools
- ❖ Basic sewing supplies

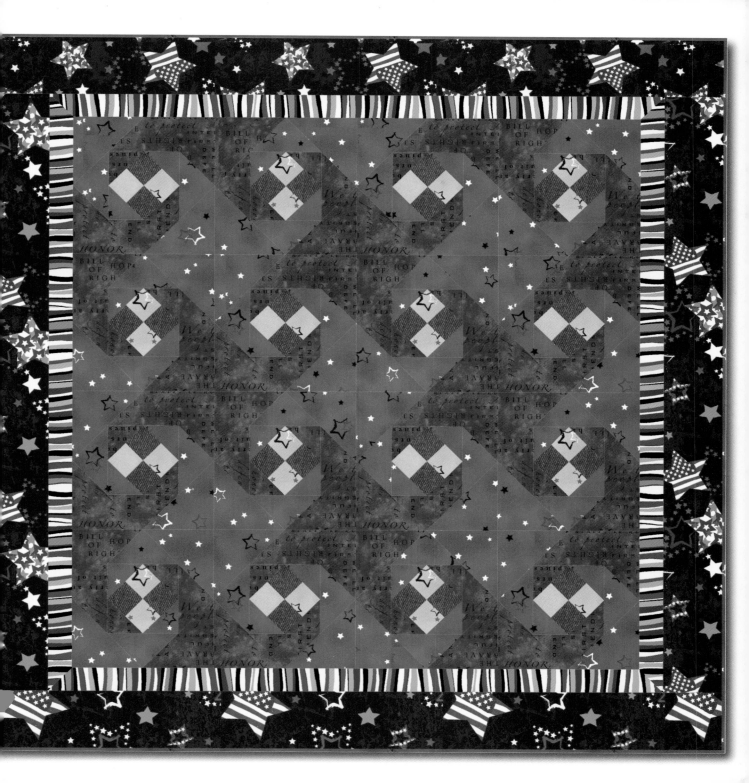

CUTTING

Label all pieces with the letters assigned. They will be used throughout the instructions.

From the light blue star print, cut
- 2 A/D strips 2⅝" x 42"

From the red texture, cut
- 2 B/C strips 2⅝" x 42"

From the medium blue print, cut
- 2 strips 3⅞" x 42"; recut into (16) 3⅞" squares, then cut each square in half diagonally to make 32 E/F triangles
- 2 strips 5⅛" x 42"; recut into (16) 5⅛" squares, then cut each square in half diagonally to make 32 I/J triangles
- 3 strips 6⅞" x 42"; recut into (16) 6⅞" squares, then cut each square in half diagonally to make 32 M/N triangles

From the red star print, cut
- 2 strips 3⅞" x 42"; recut into (16) 3⅞" squares, then cut each square in half diagonally to make 32 G/H triangles
- 2 strips 5⅛" x 42"; recut into (16) 5⅛" squares, then cut each square in half diagonally to make 32 K/L triangles
- 3 strips 6⅞" x 42"; recut into (16) 6⅞" squares, then cut each square in half diagonally to make 32 O/P triangles
- 7 strips 2¼" x 42" for binding

From the stripe, cut
- 6 strips 2½" x 42" for inner border

From the navy star print, cut
- 6 strips 6½" x 42" for outer border

From the backing fabric, cut
- 2 pieces 72" long

MAKING THE SNAIL'S TRAIL BLOCKS

Use a ¼" seam allowance throughout unless otherwise instructed.

1. Sew a light blue A/D strip lengthwise together with a red B/C strip. Press seam toward the B/C strip. Repeat to make a second strip set. Crosscut the strip sets into (32) 2⅝" segments.

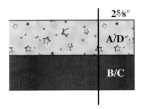

2. Join two segments to complete a block center. Press seam to one side. Repeat to make 16 block centers total.

Make 16

3. Refer to Building the Block on page 6, steps 4—7, to make (16) 12$^{1}/_{2}$" x 12$^{1}/_{2}$" Snail's Trail blocks.

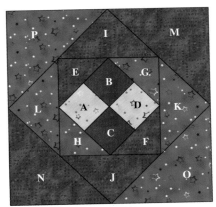

Make 16

COMPLETING THE QUILT CENTER

1. Sew four blocks together to make a block row. Press seams to one side. Repeat to make four rows total. *Note: For help with matching the triangle corners from block to block, refer to Build It Better on page 24.*

2. Join the block rows to complete the 48$^{1}/_{2}$" x 48$^{1}/_{2}$" quilt center. Press seams in one direction. (Refer to the Quilt Assembly Diagram on page 18.)

3. Sew the 2$^{1}/_{2}$" x 42" stripe strips short ends together to make a long strip. Cut into four 58" strips. Refer to Mitered Corners on page 27 to sew the stripe strips to the sides of the quilt center.

4. Sew the 6$^{1}/_{2}$" x 42" navy star print strips short ends together to make a long strip. Cut into two 52$^{1}/_{2}$" and two 64$^{1}/_{2}$" strips. Sew the shorter strips to opposite sides and the longer strips to the remaining sides of the quilt center to complete the quilt top. Press seams toward the strips. *Note: Refer to Finishing Basics on page 26 for information about cutting border strips.*

FINISHING THE QUILT

1. Remove the selvage edges from the backing pieces. Sew the pieces together down the length with a $^{1}/_{2}$" seam allowance. Trim the sides to make a 72" x 72" backing piece. Press seam open.

2. Refer to Finishing Basics to layer, quilt, and bind your quilt.

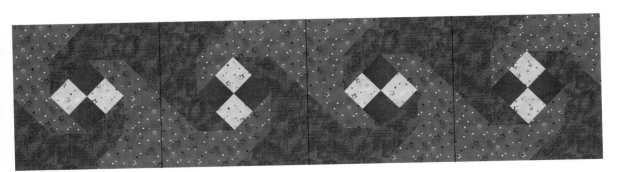

Build It Better

Rather not do mitered corners on the stripe border? Cut the long strip into two 48½" strips and two 52½" strips (see Finishing Basics on page 26 for information about measuring for and cutting border strips). Then sew the shorter strips to opposite sides and the longer strips to the remaining sides of the quilt center.

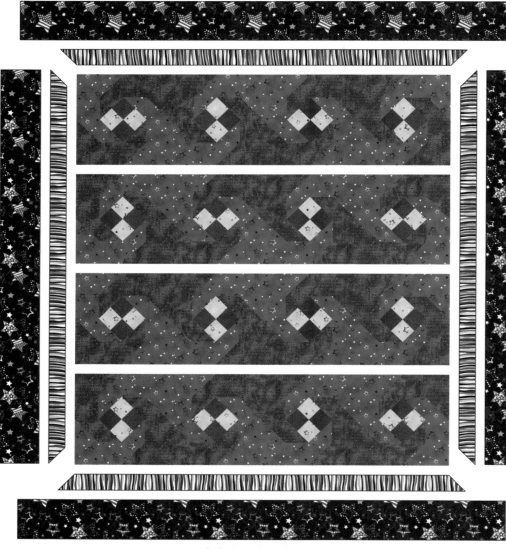

Quilt Assembly Diagram

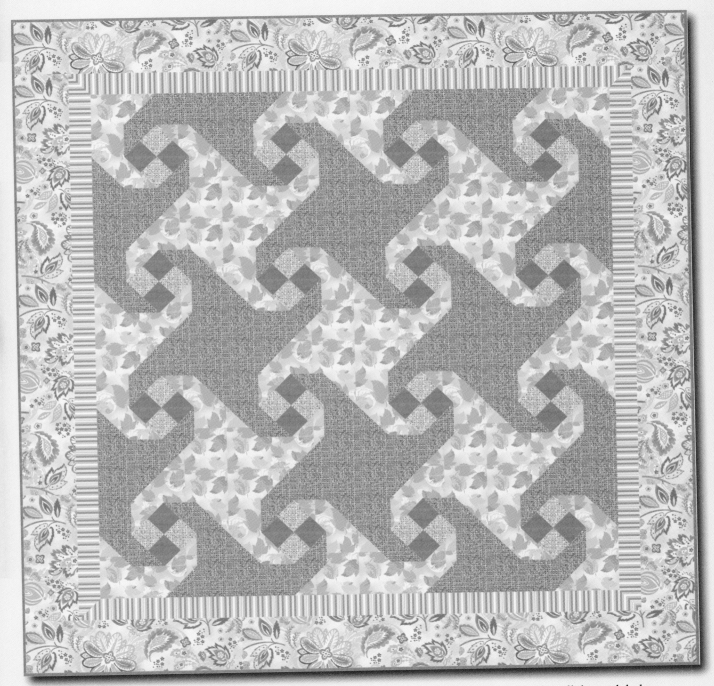

Contrasts in fabric make the traditional setting of this quilt really sing! Near-solids and prints, lights and darks, warms and cools—any combination gives definition to this interlocking design.

Line Dancing

Four fabrics in only two colors make a quarter-turn from block to block to form the twisting, turning rows of this quilt. A subtle pieced border rounds out the blended effect.

Finished Quilt Size: 65" x 73$1/2$"
Finished Block Size: 8$1/2$" x 8$1/2$"
Number of Blocks: 42
Skill Level: Intermediate

MATERIALS
All yardages are based on 42"-wide fabric.

- ❖ 2$1/4$ yards of sage green floral
- ❖ 1$1/2$ yards of sage green print
- ❖ 1$3/8$ yards of yellow/sage print
- ❖ 1$3/8$ yards of yellow texture
- ❖ 4$3/4$ yards of backing fabric
- ❖ 73" x 82" piece of batting
- ❖ Thread to match fabrics
- ❖ Rotary cutting tools
- ❖ Basic sewing supplies

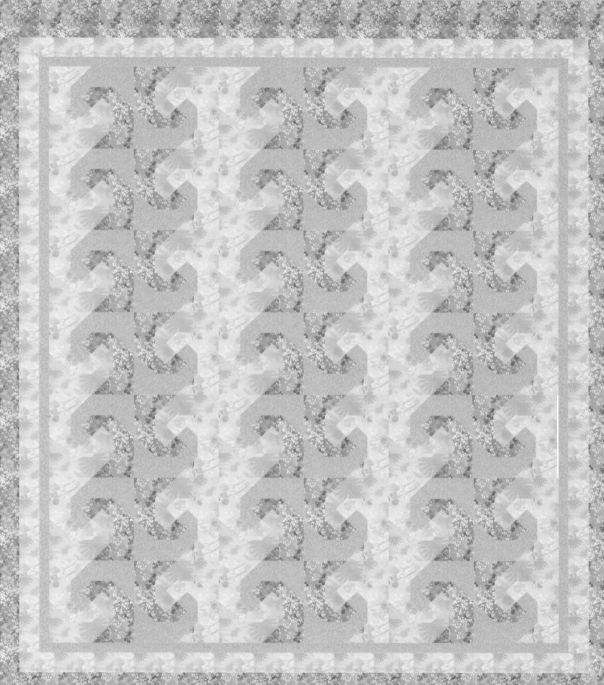

CUTTING

Label all pieces with the letters assigned. They will be used throughout the instructions.

From the sage green floral, cut
- 2 A strips 2" x 42"
- 2 strips 3" x 42"; recut into (21) 3" squares, then cut each square in half diagonally to make 42 E triangles
- 3 strips 3⅞" x 42"; recut into (21) 3⅞" squares, then cut each square in half diagonally to make 42 I triangles
- 3 strips 5⅛" x 42"; recut into (21) 5⅛" squares, then cut each square in half diagonally to make 42 M triangles
- 7 strips 4½" x 42" for outer border

From the sage green print, cut
- 2 B strips 2" x 42"
- 2 strips 3" x 42"; recut into (21) 3" squares, then cut each square in half diagonally to make 42 G triangles
- 3 strips 3⅞" x 42"; recut into (21) 3⅞" squares, then cut each square in half diagonally to make 42 K triangles
- 3 strips 5⅛" x 42"; recut into (21) 5⅛" squares, then cut each square in half diagonally to make 42 O triangles
- 6 strips 1½" x 42" for inner border

From the yellow/sage print, cut
- 2 C strips 2" x 42"
- 2 strips 3" x 42"; recut into (21) 3" squares, then cut each square in half diagonally to make 42 H triangles
- 3 strips 3⅞" x 42"; recut into (21) 3⅞" squares,

then cut each square in half diagonally to make 42 L triangles
- 3 strips 5⅛" x 42"; recut into (21) 5⅛" squares, then cut each square in half diagonally to make 42 P triangles
- 2 strips 2½" x 42"; recut into (60) 2½" Q squares

From the yellow texture, cut
- 2 D strips 2" x 42"
- 2 strips 3" x 42"; recut into (21) 3" squares, then cut each square in half diagonally to make 42 F triangles
- 3 strips 3⅞" x 42"; recut into (21) 3⅞" squares, then cut each square in half diagonally to make 42 J triangles
- 3 strips 5⅛" x 42"; recut into (21) 5⅛" squares, then cut each square in half diagonally to make 42 N triangles
- 2 strips 2½" x 42"; recut into (60) 2½" R squares

From the backing fabric, cut
- 2 pieces 82" long

MAKING THE SNAIL'S TRAIL BLOCKS

Use a ¼" seam allowance throughout unless otherwise instructed.

1. Sew a green floral A strip lengthwise together with a green print B strip. Press seam toward the B strip. Repeat to make a second strip set. Crosscut the strip sets into (42) 2" AB segments.

2. Sew a yellow/sage C strip lengthwise together with a yellow texture D strip. Press seams toward the C strip. Repeat to make a second strip set. Crosscut the strip sets into (42) 2" CD segments.

3. Sew an AB segment to a CD segment to complete a block center. Press seam to one side. Repeat to make 42 block centers total.

A	B
C	D

Make 42

4. Refer to Building the Block on page 6, steps 4-7, to make (42) 9" x 9" Snail's Trail blocks.

Make 42

COMPLETING THE QUILT CENTER

1. Sew six blocks together to make a block row. Press seams to one side. Repeat to make seven rows total, pressing the seams in four rows to the left and in three rows to the right.

2. Join the block rows to complete the 51 1/2" x 60" quilt center. Press seams in one direction. (Refer to the Quilt Assembly Diagram on page 24.)

3. Stitch the 1 1/2" x 42" sage green print strips short ends together to make a long strip. Cut into two 60" strips and two 53 1/2" strips. Sew the longer strips to the long sides and the shorter strips to the top and bottom of the quilt center. Press seams toward the strips. *Note: Refer to Finishing Basics on page 26 for information about cutting border strips.*

4. Sew 16 yellow/sage print Q squares alternately together with 15 yellow texture R squares to make a side strip. Press seams toward the Q squares. Repeat to make a second side strip. Trim the strips to 62" long, cutting an equal amount off each end of the strips.

Side–Make 2

Top/Bottom–Make 2

5. Stitch the side strips to the long sides of the quilt center. Press seams toward the strips.

6. Sew 15 yellow texture R squares alternately together with 14 yellow/sage print Q squares to make the top strip. Press seams toward the Q squares. Repeat to make the bottom strip. Trim the strips to 57 1/2" long, cutting an equal amount off each end of the strips.

7. Stitch the strips to the top and bottom of the quilt center. Press seams toward the strips.

8. Sew the 4 1/2" x 42" sage green floral strips short ends together to make a long strip. Cut into two 66" and two 65 1/2" strips. Sew the longer strips to the long sides and the shorter strips to the top and bottom of the quilt center to complete the quilt top. Press seams toward the strips.

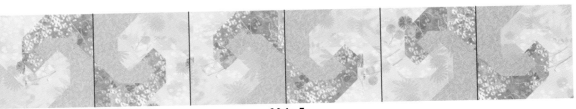

Make 7

FINISHING THE QUILT

1. Remove the selvage edges from the backing pieces. Sew the pieces together down the length with a $1/2$" seam allowance. Trim the sides to make a 73" x 82" backing piece. Press seam open.

2. Refer to Finishing Basics to layer, quilt, and bind your quilt.

Build It Better

Having trouble matching the angled seams and triangle corners when joining the blocks in rows? Place two blocks right sides together, matching O to N and M to P. Stick a pin straight through the corner of the K triangle on the green side and through the corner of the L triangle on the yellow side of the block. Bring the blocks together on the pin so that the two corners are aligned. Pin to hold the blocks together and remove the pin in the triangle corners. Be sure your stitching goes straight across the very tip of the L/K triangles. A perfect match!

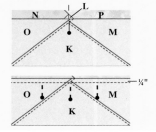

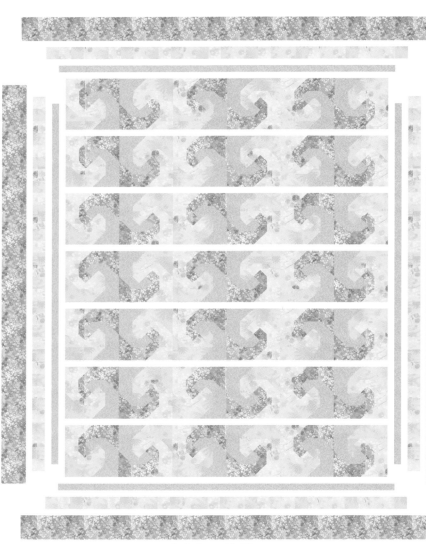

Quilt Assembly Diagram

The subtle pieced border of the original quilt becomes bold in this version of *Line Dancing*. The defined differences in the value and color of these fabrics give each "arm" of the block a distinct shape.

Finishing Basics

ADDING BORDERS

Borders are an important part of your quilt. They add another design element, and act much like a picture frame to complement and support the center.

There are two basic types of borders—butted corners and mitered corners. Butted corners are the most common. For this technique, border strips are stitched to opposite sides of the quilt center, pressed, and then strips are sewn to the remaining sides. Mitered corners are often used to continue a pattern around the corners; for example, the stripe in a fabric or a pieced border design.

 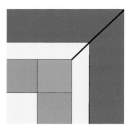

Butted corners   **Mitered corners**

Lengths are given for the borders in the individual quilt instructions. In most cases, fabric-width strips are joined to make a strip long enough to cut two side strips and top and bottom strips. Because of differences in piecing and pressing, your quilt center may differ slightly in size from the mathematically exact

size used to determine the border lengths. Before cutting the strips for butted corners, refer to the instructions given here to measure for lengths to fit your quilt center. For mitered borders, extra length is already included in the sizes given in the instructions to make it easier to stitch the miters. It should be enough to allow for any overall size differences.

BUTTED CORNERS

1. Press the quilt center. Arrange it on a flat surface with the edges straight.

2. Fold the quilt in half lengthwise, matching edges and corners. Finger-press the center fold to make a crease. Unfold.

3. Measure along the center ceased line to determine the length of the quilt center.

 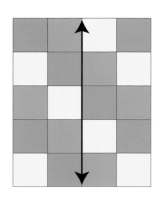

Fold in half

4. Cut two strips this length.

5. Fold the strips in half across the width and finger-press to make a crease.

6. Place a strip right sides together on one long edge of the quilt center, aligning the creased center of the strip with the center of the long edge. Pin in place at the center. Align the ends of the strips with the top and bottom edges of the quilt center. Pin in place at each end.

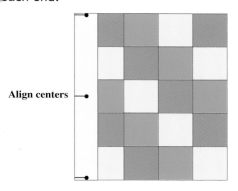

Align centers

7. Pin between the ends and center, easing any fullness, if necessary.

8. Stitch the border to the quilt center. Press.

9. Repeat on the remaining long edge.

10. Fold the quilt in half across the width and crease to mark the center. Unfold. Measure along the creased line to determine the width of the bordered quilt center.

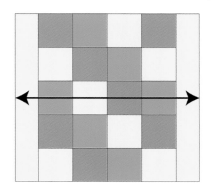

11. Cut two strips this length.

12. Repeat steps 5—9 on the top and bottom edges of the quilt center.

MITERED CORNERS

1. Prepare the border strips as directed in the individual pattern.

2. Make a mark 1/4" on each side of the quilt corners.

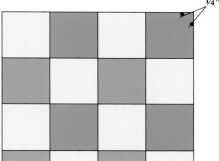

¼"

3. Center the border strips on each side of the quilt top and pin in place. Stitch in place, stopping and locking stitches at the 1/4" mark at each corner.

4. Fold the quilt top in half diagonally with wrong sides together. Arrange two border ends right sides together.

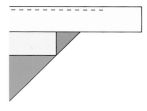

5. Mark a 45°angle line from the locked stitching on the border to the outside edge of the border.

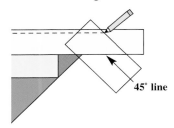

45° line

6. Stitch on the marked line, starting exactly at the locked stitch. Trim seam allowance to 1/4".

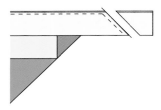

7. Press the mitered corner seam open and the seam between the border and the rest of the quilt toward the border.

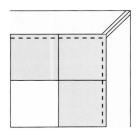

8. Repeat these steps on each corner of the quilt.

LAYERING, BASTING & QUILTING

You may choose to do your own quilting or take your projects to a machine quilter. Be sure that your backing and batting are at least 4" wider and 4" longer on each side of the quilt top. The size needed is given in the Materials list for each project.

If you would like to quilt your own project, there are many good books about hand and machine quilting. Check with your quilting friends or at your local quilt shop for recommendations. Here are the basic steps to do your own quilting:

1. Mark the quilt top with a quilting design, if desired.

2. Place the backing right side down on a flat surface. Place the batting on top. Center the quilt top right side up on top of the batting. Smooth all the layers. Thread-baste, pin, or spray-baste the layers together to hold while quilting.

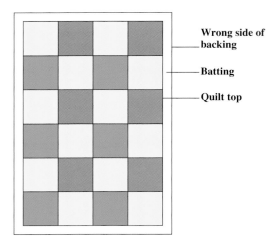

Wrong side of backing

Batting

Quilt top

3. Quilt the layers by hand or machine.

4. When quilting is finished, trim the batting and backing even with the quilted top.

BINDING

The patterns in this book include plenty of fabric to cut either 2¹/4" or 2¹/2" wide strips for straight-grain, double-fold binding. In some cases, a wider binding or bias binding is needed because of a specific edge treatment; extra yardage is included when necessary.

PREPARING STRAIGHT-GRAIN, DOUBLE-FOLD BINDING

1. Cut strips as directed for the individual pattern. Remove selvage edges.

2. Place the ends of two binding strips right sides together at a right angle. Mark a line from inside corner to inside corner. Stitch on the marked line. Trim seam allowance to ¹/4".

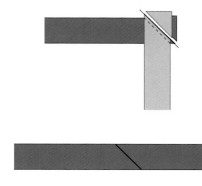

3. Repeat step 2 to join all binding strips into one long strip. Press seams to one side. Fold the strip in half lengthwise with wrong sides together and press.

PREPARING DOUBLE-FOLD BIAS BINDING

1. Cut an 18" x 42" strip from the binding fabric.

2. Place the 45˚ angle line of a rotary ruler on one edge of the strip. Trim off one corner of the strip.

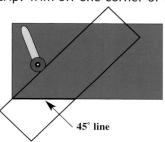

45° line

3. Cut binding strips in the width specified in the pattern from the angled end of the strip.

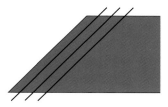

4. Each strip will be approximately 25" long. Cut strips to total the length needed for the pattern, repeating steps 1 and 2 if needed.

5. Align the ends of two strips with right sides together. Stitch ¹/4" from the ends.

6. Repeat to join all binding strips into one long strip. Press seams to one side.

ADDING THE BINDING

1. Leaving a 6"-8" tail and beginning several inches from a corner, align the raw edges of the binding with the edge of the quilt. Stitch along the edge with a $1/4$" seam allowance, locking stitches at the beginning.

2. Stop $1/4$" from the first corner and lock stitching. Remove the quilt from your machine. Turn the quilt so the next edge is to your right. Fold the binding end up and then back down so the fold is aligned with the previous edge of the quilt and the binding is aligned with the edge to your right. Starting at the edge of the quilt, stitch the binding to the next corner.

3. Repeat step 2 to attach binding to the rest of the quilt, stopping stitching 6"–8" from the starting point and locking stitches.

4. Unfold the ends of the strips. Press flat. About halfway between the stitched ends, fold the beginning strip up at a right angle. Press. Fold the ending strip down at a right angle, with the folded edge butted against the fold of the beginning end. Press.

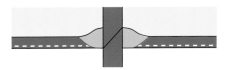

5. Trim each end $1/4$" from creased fold. Place the trimmed ends right sides together. Pin to hold. Stitch $1/4$" from the ends. Press the seam allowance open.

6. Refold the strip in half. Press. Arrange the strip on the edge of the quilt and stitch in place to finish the binding.

7. Fold the edge of the binding over the raw edges to the back of the quilt. Hand stitch in place, covering the machine stitches and mitering the corners.

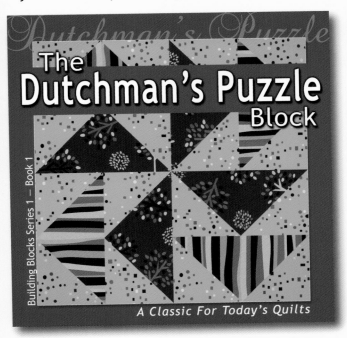

The
Dutchman's Puzzle
Block

Building Blocks Series 1 – Book 1

A Classic For Today's Quilts

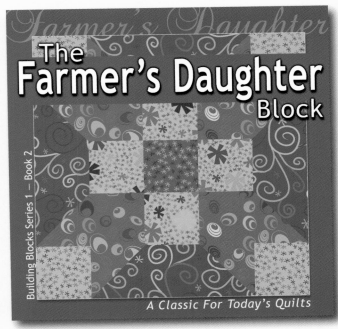

The
Farmer's Daughter
Block

Building Blocks Series 1 – Book 2

A Classic For Today's Quilts

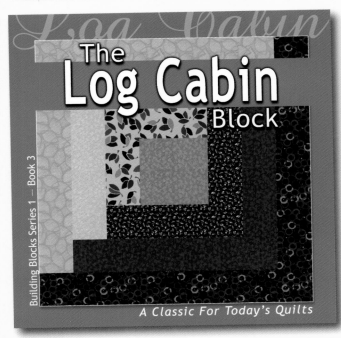

The
Log Cabin
Block

Building Blocks Series 1 – Book 3

A Classic For Today's Quilts

The
Snail's Trail
Block

Building Blocks Series 1 – Book 4

A Classic For Today's Quilts

Books 5-8 →

COLLECT THEM ALL! Look for the complete Building Blocks Series 1 Books 1–8 at your local quilt shop, favorite book store, or order www.allamericancrafts.com.

The
Wild Goose Chase
Block

Building Blocks Series 1 – Book 5

A Classic For Today's Quilts

The
Gentleman's Fancy
Block

Building Blocks Series 1 – Book 6

A Classic For Today's Quilts

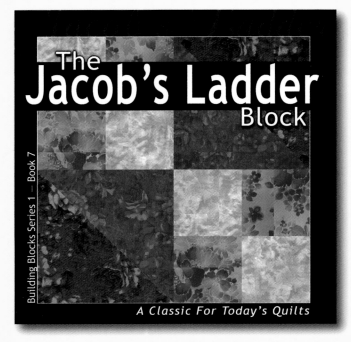

The
Jacob's Ladder
Block

Building Blocks Series 1 – Book 7

A Classic For Today's Quilts

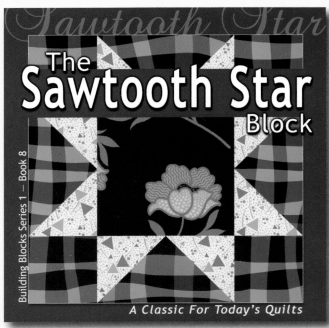

The
Sawtooth Star
Block

Building Blocks Series 1 – Book 8

A Classic For Today's Quilts